A Kalmus Classic Edition

Arcangelo

CORELLI

LA FOLIA

FOR VIOLIN AND PIANO

K 04409

Kalmus

La Folia.
Variations sérieuses.

A. CORELLI.

La Folia.
Variations sérieuses.

Violin.

A. CORELLI.

BELWIN/MILLS PUBLISHING CORP.

Violin.

Violin.

Violin.